A Bride of Narrow Escape

For Sarah,
dear heart —
with love,
Paulann
APRIL 2006

Northwest Poetry Series

A Bride of Narrow Escape

Paulann Petersen

Cloudbank Books
Brownsville, Oregon

First Edition

Library of Congress Cataloging in Publication Data

Paulann Petersen, 1942 —
A Bride of Narrow Escape

ISBN: 0-9665018-8-8

Library of Congress Control Number: 2005935666

Cloudbank Books is an imprint of
Bedbug Press, P.O. Box 39, Brownsville, OR 97327

Cover art by Mimi Shapiro
Cover design and book design by Brandon Conn
Cloudbank Books logo is a carving by Julie Hagan Bloch from
Haunting Us With His Love by David Samuel Bloch.
Text set in Bookman
Printed at Thomson-Shore, Inc., Dexter, MI

for Lawson Fusao Inada,
mentor, master story-teller

for Ken,
with gratitude

CONTENTS

I. The Home of Your Life

II. Residues

III. An Animal's Making

I.

The Home
of Your Life

There is a thing or two
I know: to speak the story
as it unfolds,
to sleep with the animal
dark and breathing
against my face,
to remember my heart
can do only this: give
and take and give
what is never
its own.

A VAPOR, IT RISES AT WAKING

Here, you are no age,
none at all. The tense is ever
present, *is* is all there is, you are
simply, presently you.

Your face—if you could
see its calm, or knit of puzzlement,
knot of fear—is indeed your face,
the same moon of shadowed flesh
you lift into the air,
not the mirror's flat image
waiting to catch you off-guard
regardless of your pose.

The house you find
yourself wandering in
is the home of your life,
both new and familiar.
Each doorknob, each knicknack
uncanny yet true.
The child-fingers still alive
inside your hands
remember each shape.

You see your mother—
immutably dead—
stir and smile. Her lips
defy all law to form
a sound so longed for, so clear
it disappears. What rises
from your body at waking
is simply her voice speaking a word
she chose at your birth,
breathing out your name.

MY FATHER, HARD AT THE WORK OF EARLY SUMMER

So ripe, a mere rap
from his knuckles split them
clear open—those watermelons
too primed with flesh and seed
to be carried from their vines
and laid on a pickup's bed.

With his open hand, he plunged
into each broken melon's center,
lifting to his mouth the heart
running in rivulets down his arm.

So said my father to me
when I was no longer a girl,
not yet a woman. So he said
of that summer when he was
no father, no child, no man.

Cool, wet, sweet: too much
to refuse. Just my age, fourteen—
savoring his first work for pay—
he could not turn his back
on those heat-wavered fields,
leaving that much red untouched.

MAINTAIN

A living room window undrapes itself
to frame the slant of winter rain
falling through stark-limbed trees.
Wallpaper sports the repetitions
of exotic vines that signal
everyday taste in the late 40's.

My father is below, in the basement
where his tools wait—sharpened,
cleaned with steel wool and a drop of oil,
hanging from hooks on pegboard.
He's a working man who's handy at home,
his workbench—edged with a vise
and wood-clamps—making a long ell
near our sawdust-burning furnace.

It was August when the truck
pulled into our driveway to thread
its chute into the basement window
propped open with a stick.
Then the truck lifted its blocky bed
in a high tilt and dumped its load
of fresh sawdust into our basement's corner.
Pouring in: that coarse dust, leftover
from lumber ripped, planed, milled.
The amber debris of trees,
salvaged for heat.

This day is cold, the furnace lit.
Lifting his shovel from where
it leans against one of the furnace's
giant octopus arms, my father fills the hopper.
With each scoop, the high, resin-sweet pile
sifts down to erase what he's done.

HIS MAP, UNFOLDING

The map my father unfolds for me
in my dream is unmistakably
a constellation. Bold, intricate—
outline of a walking man
made from stars, a fine line
connecting each to each.
Limbs, trunk, mouth and eyes—
all of him drawn with stars.
And from his navel, place most human,
rays of light shoot out
like long spokes from a hub.

My father's hand motions me
closer so I see that the stars
of this sidereal body
also mark intersections.
The outline of this man's shape
is part of a roadmap, too.
Its highways fork and cross,
spreading their star-lines
along the quiet green
of the paper's creased terrain.

Birthplace of countless roads,
the navel's glittering hub
rises distinct from the map's surface
where rivers and lakes and oceans
keep serenities of blue.

My father's map begins in the air
and breath of a dream.
Godlike. Thing of heaven,
a walk across the sky,
his map ends here, on ground,
place of the body's work and rest.

RESTORER

—for Paul Whitman (1912–1988)

Touching the world, my father
worked its workable surfaces
with patience. A paint-slathered chair became
an object for his slow ministration:
platform rocker, each rail, style, and rung
the product of a lathe's spin.
All the chair's wood was turned,
incised. Every inch clogged
with three coats of thick enamel.
Nothing to do—short of resignation—
but remove the paint without
sanding the chair away.

With emery cloth cut into thin ribbons,
he looped a strip into a turning's groove,
and began. Each hand grasping an end,
his arms two slow pistons,
he dragged the gritty strip to and fro
against the surface, like a pulley,
wearing paint away.
                              After his workday,
night after night in our basement,
the brown gave way to a red that gave way
to dirt-green. The green gave way
to turn-of-a-century varnish—
a last, thin darkness he rubbed
quickly to dust.

Quarter-inch by quarter-inch,
maple emerged—like a tree he'd spotted
far in the distance, in shade,
then walked toward. Steady footsteps nearing
a copse now opened by sun.

LIVING IN PAIN

Money is useless here.
Whatever he pulls from his pocket
is turned away. No door
exists to a place of welcome,
only windows through which he peers

into other lives.
A woman bends to the shape
of routine, the food she prepares
having so much smell
or so little smell, it consumes

all the air either way.
Sparrows perch in trees
with unfamiliar sharpness,
their markings too brown, too gray.
They sing in tongues.

He remembers the grandfather,
tongue-tied at birth,
how a doctor cut the membrane
that held his speech.
Here, in this foreign place,

this country of the body
where everyone is native born,
he is the tongue-tied,
waiting for a knife
to free his voice.

SCOUR

On the day my father can leave
the hospital, the retching pain
having left him alone
for now, he asks a favor.
Clean his false teeth.
He loosens them from behind
his lips, drops them into
my outstretched hand.
Warm from his blood, spittle-strings
stick to them—their gums entirely
too pink, teeth purposely
not too white.

I squeeze DentuCreme
onto his toothbrush, and under
the faucet's falling stream, scrub
hard—to clear away
the spit, his slick
mouth-leavings.
Each tooth
looks too small, unequal
to its job. Never before have I touched
what lives inside my father's mouth.

Still warm. Now I might somehow see
in two years he'll be dead.
But all I'm sure of is this:
only animal jawbones
I've seen in the woods
are this perfect—scoured
clean by weather and hunger.
From them, each long tooth
can be worked out, then slid back without
a trace of undoing.

A LAST COOL, SWEET THING

This is the story beyond
my telling. I can say it only once.
This father is dying, and I
am his daughter. His stomach's fluid
bubbles up in his throat.
His belly is so swollen it strains
the same hospital gown
that collapses in folds around
his ravaged arms and chest.
His scrotum, where the cancer began,
is a huge sac, bruised and angry
between his legs, his penis
has nearly vanished.

I'm the one who tells him
what the doctor has said. This time
he won't go home.
I've been expecting that, he says,
eyes wide, steady. That's all.
I have no words for reply.

Nothing to eat now. Only water
and the icy-bright popsicle halves
a nurse brings. He turns one on his lips,
juice collecting in his mouth,
the tip softening to slush
on his tongue. One hand holds
the wooden stick, the other hand free
to reach for the button that feeds him—
at each press of his thumb—
drops of morphine. Balm.

He calls me closer.
*You know your mama's going to need
a lot of care, don't you?*
and smiles, murmuring *I knew
you'd say that*, when I answer
I do. I will.
Smacking his lips in play,
eyes gone dreamy with narcotic, he says,
Here, Baby, do this for me,
and I stand for hours
bringing a popsicle half to his mouth—
his lips and tongue darkening to
the purple of wine.

STONE

Eighteen, I once imagined
my parents dead. Vanished.
Their too ordinary ways
swept away, leaving me
sculpted stone,
wrapped in a sheen of loss.
Shameless, I touched my tongue
to a salt lick of pretended grief.

Now my own children
are old enough
to dream my death.
My father's ashes wait
in their cardboard coffin.
My mother waits like a stone
to hear from me,
forgetting we spoke
only moments ago.

Salt is the flavor
of my own body's wellings.
My dreams rise—ordinary,
vanishing—bereft of life
or death. I begin
and end each day alone.
Loss wraps its heavy
garment around me,
a skin of stone.

FALSE SPRING

Mother, this day is so beautiful
I almost forget you are
dying your long slow death.
The anniversary of Daddy's death-day
has come and gone, buried in this month's
sleet-ridden beginnings,
left behind in the winter they swore
you would never survive.
Late March, and the day rises
clear, windless, with enough heat
thrown down from the sky
to pass for summer.

Today the mountains grow
beyond familiarity, flaring their white sides
to the sun, looming up as the temples
they are. Airplanes ease through the sky,
pursuing routes so unhindered by clouds,
their metallic bellies shine
like prayers on their way
to a merciful god.

At ground level, a bumblebee,
round and inky, fat as tenacity,
fumbles along. Stunned by its own
unexpected motion, it lumbers across
the feathery leaves of fennel
growing unbidden by the front steps—
what you would have called
a volunteer. Here, still—a boon
that weathered the hard winter through—
unfurling its dark, candy scent
into the sun-struck air.

You lie rigid and blank-eyed
in a care-giver's extra room,
responding only to a spoon
on your cracking lips, to any food
sweet or salty in your mouth.
One rote motion left to you,
one blind tropism. No more. Yet today
I praise that you live on,
this welling of my gratitude
as unwilled as some wide-faced flower's
turning to follow the sun.
Unexpected as this bloom of heat
refusing to settle for anything
less than alive.

DUTY

—for Grace Whitman (1914–1995)

Twice a week my mother
went down in the basement to iron
her white uniforms—starched,
dampened, and waiting in a bundle
by the ironing board. First, collar, yoke,
waistband, cuffs and hem. Then the lengths
of wrinkled skirt and sleeve that remained.
And to finish: a last touch-up
to the collar's stiff points.

I watched as she pressed heat
into each flattened nurse's cap,
where an embroidered circle held
the initials that told where she'd trained.
SMH, in curves of blue. St. Mary's Hospital.

That meant San Francisco, and the nuns
who had, for three years, commandeered her life.
On her shift, when anything near her
had gone amiss—an autoclave turned on
and forgotten, a pan of instruments left to boil
black and dry—she'd been made to take,
standing rigid and wordless,
the ear-scorching blame.
Then, guilty or not, she'd been taught to reply
Yes, Sister, Thank you, Sister,
in gratitude for what the good nun
had pointed out. But that had been years ago,
was of smaller account—her easy smile told me—
than a young daughter could know.
Harsh or not, the nuns had taught her
to be a good nurse.

From what she carried, crisp and spotless,
up the dark twist of stairs,
she picked a uniform and cap,
still warm from the iron.
White hose. White, polished
duty shoes, their laces scrubbed clean.
The reverie of heat—
starch-scented, bleach-scented steam—
was gone. Time to go to work.

LANE CHANGE

A snapshot glance over my shoulder,
and I make my move, quick, thinking
how easy, how simple to
not see, to hit, be hit: the blindside
slash of metal, of glass,
my flesh driven back into the sharpness
of my own teeth and bones.
Smashed just like that,
and maybe not even a stop

for pain. Maybe my mind
plucks me away from my done-for
body, lets me think I live on,
still driving the now gone-to-scrap car
onto the arc of bridge that each day routes me
home. Driving up, over the river's sheen,
cresting above midflow, then down
onto the other side and off, until it's all
a pure coast.

Maybe my mother's last years
were such a thing. Those motionless,
voiceless days not days or nights
at all, not a senseless dragging
of flesh, not some nightmare sleep
that kept her awake enough
to chew, to swallow,
her bowels and bladder emptied
by tubes. Not that, but just
her behind the wheel,
some sun easing through the windshield,
dust whispered along the dash,

a tune she likes on the radio,
little hum harboring somewhere
in her throat. Here comes the approach
to the bridge, and another driver stops
long enough to let her into the line
of crossing cars. A wave of thanks,

then a slow climb to the part
she likes best, at the bridge's crest.
There she can glimpse a mountain's point
and a river's mirror length,
the part that could just as well last forever
if anyone bothered to ask her.
Up and over the narrow span—that one drive
she could do in her sleep,
the easy one, home.

REPRIEVE

Through the phone a woman's voice asks
if I am my name, and when I answer yes,
tells me she'll put my mother on the line.
A crazy lightning sheers through my pulse
as I say *my mother?* not thinking of
little miracles, windows of clarity—
surely not that unheard of—
when the random notes of Alzheimer's
might suddenly form a pure chord,
sweet sound of my mother saying
I don't want to be any bother,
but come get me, I need to go home.
But quickly: the woman's confusion in the face
of my confusion, her stumbled apology.
She doesn't usually work this part of the floor,
she got mixed up, but my mom's just fine, actually
she's placing a call for my mother's roommate,
and grabbed the wrong name and number,
oh dear, she can see how the call would be a shock
and she's sorry, really sorry, but my mother
is fine, doing just fine.
                Hanging up,
I'm stunned, wishing I'd said without hesitation
Yes, put her on, wanting to believe
that with faith, whole and unwavering,
I'd have heard my mother—
her voice finding something on her mind,
maybe slow and faltering, but yes, just fine—
heard her speak to me one more time.

REMAINS

I take my parents
into my hands, I let them go.
My father's ashes are dark,
almost black. My mother's pale,
not quite white. The color of bone
alike, as if they'd shared
a single frame.

Ash taken away by wind
lays a glinting film on the sea.
Bits of bone roll coarse between
my forefinger and thumb. Gone.
Now my hands are roughened
by the grit of my parents' skin,
hair, muscle, blood.
Their bodies settle on me.

Such is the mineral world—
stone, silt and salt,
gold beaten so thin it's merely
a sheen, silver rolled
sheer enough to be eaten,
gleam and all.
The dust of my parents
so fine on my hands
it barely shadows my palms.

II.

Residues

What's left when a figure's gone
is more than simply a home minus
what's been taken away. Remaining
is every possibility, each move that
figure didn't know enough to make.

COLLISION

In the corner of my dreaming eye
I spot a car—
speeding streak of red

intent on me—in time
to hit the brakes, breaking the sweet
escape of a Sunday's

stolen nap. Thunderclap
of hairline luck
slams me back. Alive and it's

still Sunday,
the day I should see
my mother who's been stalled between

dying and death
for two motionless, unspeaking
unspeakable years,

her closed-eye
then open-eyed hours
alike: one great unshaken sleep

whose dreams or dreamlessness
lie beyond detection,
beyond my most fervent call.

The phone call I more than half hoped
would interrupt my nap—
one from the man I'm sure

isn't right for me—
still hasn't come. I have no more notion
of love and me and men

than I did at seventeen, divining lyrics
of some dreamy song,
mining its words for a clue.

That whole batch
of hotcakes I ate too fast,
a breakaway breakfast because I seldom

fix for just myself, is still
a dull clump
caught in my chest. I'm stuck

with stubborn lodgers
in my body, struck with the thud
of what awaits,

but spared, yes saved and now
wildly awake—
a bride of narrow escape.

A TAMING

The bride across the street,
sleek-haired, her fingernails
dipped in red—ran to me flushed
from screaming, awry with fear.
A bird was thrashing, flinging against
pale walls, the picture window,
draperies of her living room.
She was stop-heart
afraid of its frenzied and slow
disintegration, the feathers loosed
and wafting, its refusal
to find the open door.

Her rough boned, no-longer-a-bride
neighbor, I would catch what she couldn't
bring her finely wrought self
to touch. I would carry it outside,
buoy it home to leafy branches,
into a swath of expanding air.
My fingers long, hands big enough
for its wings to stay safely
pressed along its sides—
heart beating as wildly against
my startled palms
as wilderness itself
held still.

SALVAGE

From a dead snow goose,
its breast already taken down
to a hollow chamber of bone,
he'd once watched me take a whole wing,
then carry my find out in one hand,
its white and black fan
lifting my arm as I walked
into the marsh wind.

A little breeze stirs this fox's coat,
the loft of its brush alive
with copper light where it lies
dead on pavement. He says once more
he'll do it. All he needs is the word.
With his penknife, *easy*, for me,
take the tail from this fox
so freshly hit that a wet tongue
juts from its pointed snout.

With needle-nosed pliers
I've pulled—sharply, each by each—
white feathers tipped in bronze
from the heart-faced owl we found
frozen to death in our barn. Bits of down
like some airborne seed
wafted from my palms.

Into my grandchild-hands
the furrier once placed
two foxtails, one silver, one blue,
to ripple from my first bike's handlebars.
That tattered skin at each tail's base
was gray. Dusty, soft.

Pounded into dust, he insists,
certain that cars will soon run over
this fox's glinted coat. He flushes at my refusal,
knowing well what I've taken,
will surely take again.
The furrier's only grandchild,
I didn't know then
to refuse, could not dream ahead
to this day's life, its small deaths.
Forgive me. I cannot bear
that fur's touch, its fire
rising from my hands.

UNDER THE SIGN OF A NEON WOLF

In a fur shop's triptych
of mirrors, I watch a girl
watching herself try on coats

of sable, ermine, mouton.
Her hands stroke
their ripple of hidden seams,

then wrap a string
of whole pelts snapping
jaw to tail around her shoulders.

She draws the mirrors around her too,
making a three-sided room.
Its walls are eyes reflecting her eyes—

animals lie in its corners.
At night when she's gone,
and the wolf's systolic light

flows through a window,
the soundless animals rise and move
to the edge of a red pool.

I was that child born
under the sign of a neon wolf,
one who learned to see

in a mirrored room where
eyes of glass watched every move.
I stood by a furrier's side

as he matched bundles of mink,
as his thin knife
broke into the gleaming pelts.

I learned the indelible
weight of an animal's
skin on my skin.

Through air thick with dander,
above the whir of needle machines
stitching together

those tatters of hollow bodies,
I heard the wolf outside
high above the street—

silently howling to city traffic,
head thrown back
in a curve of neon tubing.

TO LOVE HARD ENOUGH

They knot, squirm, dissolve,
drip in flames. *You like that, huh?*
says an older boy to me—one of the tall-as-a-man
neighbor boys standing nearby.

I don't say no, don't even
shake my head, having no name
for what rivets my little-girl eyes
to the apple tree branch going up in flames.
Leafless branch made bare in summer
by the gauzy embrace of something people call
a *tent*. Tent caterpillars, their fine-spun
webbing spread from twig to twig
like the work of a thousand cobby spiders.

Now they and their garment of fog are tossed
into a fire built on the neighbor's back lawn.
Burn them: branch, web, worm, eggs, all.
Let the flames take their furred life, and the half-life
of the branch just now severed from its tree,
and the half of a half-life of leaves
days ago eaten down by the caterpillars.
Take the leaves' green that's now within the wool
spun out of those wormy bodies,
the green now inside the smoke that curls,
in the liquid that drips from these flames.

My eyes smart, and I hate the older boy
who says I watch, gaze unbroken, because I love
what I see. I hate his words and know
such sight is more than fascination, is indeed—
he's right—*a love*. Love for how the world
can twist and change and flame,
then drift away. Its agony
a little smoke rising toward the trees.

FOR A SEASON'S KEEPING

After they'd rolled inside his cleaning drums—
slowly cresting, falling,
tumbled with sharp-scented sawdust
for hours, for days, for hours—

the coats hung gleaming
from lead pipe racks inside the furrier's
cold storage room.

Standing among them, cold already
through starched cotton of my dress,
sifting into my skin,
I breathed their scent—
air of a winter made in July
for creatures whose names
were words of a gypsy
strange and beautiful on my tongue.

Karakul, cony, mouton,
kolinsky, fitch, Persian lamb,
foxes of silver, foxes of blue,
marten, moleskin, lynx,
a room of animals silenced by cold.

Moving in shadow, I eased
between them, then held my body still.
Their fur pressed me from both sides,
against my arms sweet and cold,
against my face, flowing back and forth
with each pull, each release of my breath.

I closed my eyes and saw them in winter—
moving through northern snows
crossed with trails of their silent travel,
in blue-gray forests marked by the brief
plumes of their breath.

PRIMED

It was middle June
during the duration
of a month that was a wait

for each day to come,
during that summer
when I would turn teen,

when I was almost something—
way past twelve and counting.
It was the middle of day,

mid-day heat halfway
between cool and hot,
a double-handed noonday

stroke: the clock's
count of twelve
reminding me of what

I was not. Still a multiple
of two, three, four, six,
I was a mere factoring

of too many baby birthdays—
crazy to be divisible by
only myself and one.

ONSET

I'd say I don't remember it
in bloom—a chestnut agog with white clusters,
red bleeding from each
orchid-like floret. But having
said so, I'm sure I do—orchids being
a luxury easy to remember,
those Mother's Day corsages I bought
with allowance quarters tied
into a hanky's corner.

On the *to* then *fro*
between home and school,
the same route, time after time:
in spring there would have been
a week or so for me to notice
tiny blood-stained orchids
unfolding themselves across the huge tree.
That was beauty, for certain.
And surely I *did* see, although I was,
yes, hurrying on to something else.

By fall—the school again
opening and closing its doors—
burrs lay on the sidewalk, in the gutter,
each covered with spines that softened and curled
like short, springy hair.
Those spiny cases were often split. Two
stiffly-furred lips parted to reveal
a plump gleam of seed.
I was six, seven,
then thirteen—each fallen chestnut
a swollen darkness
my fingers could not resist.

MOLES

One fumbled into sunlight
so the neighbor thrust his shovel at me
saying   *Kill it   don't be a fool*
bash its head   you know
how they ruin a lawn

while I stood and stared
at its beautiful hands
digging back into earth.

But these are a different kind.
Nana said, *They're beauty marks*
be glad you have so many.
Ollie said, *You wait, someday*
a man will kiss them one by one.

Some were too suspicious.
Those a surgeon kissed
with his scalpel,
leaving my face and neck
speckled with black stitches
fine as a wren's tracks.
The sutures plucked out,
he watched my scars
redden and spread.
Then returned to get
each hard, scarlet weal,
sewing with wire
the skin that would not close.

At night I pleaded   *Go home—*
dig back to my blood,
be beautiful.

WHITE LIE

In our grade school gym—emptied of all
but its volleyball net and us three—
Miss Pappas, our 8th grade teacher,
tells my best friend Barbara
she has looks like Debbie Reynolds.
Barbara Corno. 5' 3", maybe even 5' 2",
perfectly shorter than all but
the unacceptably short boys.
Small waist, hips, shoulders, arms, feet.
Small but not too-small breasts.
Her every inch an exact
not-inch of me. Her dress size the one
I have to pass on the rack
to get to my own, despite how thin I am.
Big-boned, the salesgirls say.
Giant, beyond hope, out of control, a body
that could just as well keep on growing
until hell ices up, is what I think.
Body bent on spreading hair
over and beyond unmentionable places.
Body marking one perfectly good skin
with splatters of dark moles
like messy constellations.
What can Miss Pappas say to me, the one
light years distant from any movie star?

You're different, she tells me later. *Not cute
or pretty like them, but the dark
sultry type. More like Ava Gardner.*
A consolation. A lie I can barely
abide. So I darken with color,
take it to heart.

BRANCH LIBRARY

Each time I went there I breathed
paper and ink, lemon oil,
the weft and warp of binding cloth.
Like the slow click of a fan swinging
side to side, time went passing.
The talcum of bodies, held to a hush,
drifted out the door.

All I knew was story, pages that led
to one another, the telling of what
might be. I imagined myself
hidden away while the librarian gathered
errant books, slid them home
on their shelves. She dusted a counter,
pinned on her hat. She left.

I lived bravely on wheatpaste and water.
Snug in her chair, I watched as
a circle of light from a gooseneck lamp
rose on her desktop blotter,
an ink-shadowed lake.

My open book
launched on this surface's ripple—
I followed its pages. I read
and I read. With each turn,
a little air stirred.

GRANT COURT

In the neighborhood of my growing-up,
the street names—*Sherman, Lincoln, Grant*—
came from the U.S. History
learned only for school. On Grant Court
our curbs still held rings to tether horses—
like the ring I'd seen in the rich part of town,
dangling from an iron jockey's outstretched hand.
Negro jockey in silks, his blackened
face grinning. Lips a crayon red.
Teeth dead white.

Black, people were learning to say,
yet the skin of that forbidden boy at school
was everything but black—copper, clay, rose and ash.
His smooth, dark arms ended in
fine brown hands. A pale moon rose under
each fingernail. His palms were the satin
of an animal's soft underside,
when he held his hands
out to me, open.

Come here, over here. His voice a curling smoke.
Dance with me, just for one song. In the living room
on Grant Court, empty of my parents, of any watcher.
His dark fingers pulled the front drapes closed.
Come here, look at me, don't be afraid—one hand circling
the small of my back, the other lifted,
open and ready to take my hand rising to meet it.
*I borrowed my folks' car, I came here
special today, just for a dance with you, alone.*

My left arm curved up and around his back.
That hand, a creature finding
a life of its own, crested on his shoulder.
My other hand pressed palm to palm against his,
its white shape now a pale twin.

My body pressing his length, my eyes
closed into the shuffle of our slow dance.
Outlined on my thigh, the brief touch of his sex
was there and not there in my mind,
the musk of his skin
easing in and out with each breath.

I was the one to pull away. No kiss, no promise,
only my eyes sliding toward the drawn drapes,
the street, toward that unfamiliar sedan
he'd parked at the curb outside.
At the threat of my parents' return,
he was gone. I stayed, in that living room.
At home on a street whose name was merely
a chain of letters, *Grant Court*. Rote sound of all
I didn't understand. The only answer I knew to give
when someone asked me, *Where do you live?*

BLACK

Basic black, said mother,
dress it up or down. Gloves,
hat, a nice pin, it'll take you
anywhere. His hands weren't
black at all. Skin that began in ash
then sank to some other
dark, rubbed to pale rose
on his palms. Blackcap jelly,
Nana's favorite. Gauze sack
of crushed fruit, juice
falling drop by drop. Colored part
of town where I'd never been,
where he worked weekends
sweeping a hall after their music played.
Mark on your reputation,
said the girls' counselor.
That's all, go back to class.
Just wanted you to know people are saying
unpleasant things. Black as the
ace of spades, said Nana,
but when he danced her around the kitchen,
his knit cap on her head,
she didn't pull away.
His mother's whiteless eyes,
steady on mine: *leave my son be.*
Brown babies, screamed my mother,
an armload of brown babies.
Think of that. Think.
Pitch black, the color of sleep
within my eyes. Years of a dream
where I lie against his body, unable
to feel him enter me. The wedding invitation
I was too ashamed to send him.
Simple as that. Right there
in black and white.

THE HOUSE AT 4 A.M.

Inside, a woman and a man have been like this
for hours, maybe days, seated face to face,
the table a smooth silence between them.
They're building a palace with matchsticks—
doorways, halls, a stairwell forming slowly
with each added piece, each omission.
She imagines a room given over to feathers,
to hollow bones; he imagines a room
draped in folds of a dark skirt.

Above them a roof slopes toward its ridgeline,
toward a chimney, unfinished or crumbling,
outlined against a cloud-lit sky.
Between their hands, the structure falls.
With the sound of collapse, they can laugh,
sigh, start again, and not think about leaving.

ACRIMONY

The deepest for miles around,
that well outside the house of our marriage
gave both water and fire.
It pumped from invisible depths
an almost undrinkable brew
frothing with sulfur's yellow,
seething with gases that swelled up
under the holding tank's top until
inside faucets choked and banged,
ready to explode.
                              What could we do
but bleed off the tank? And, to that
escaping jet of pent-up fumes,
set a match. Huge blowtorch,
the tank spewed forth a six foot
spout of flame. Our fire-show
born from the same source as the means
to put it out. For us, old hat.
Still, we gasped and jumped,
taken aback by the heat
we dared to ignite.

A ONE-SIDED CONVERSATION
WITH THE MOON

Never No Regrets, you proclaim
from your throne in the night, and I reply
Get real. Get a grip on memory,
on that grip memory's got,
and tell me how you'll evict regret
from memory's street.

I don't care how you throw
your weight around, pulling the ocean's
fat waves from side to side.
I don't care how many flowers unfold
their perfume in the dark
just for you.

Don't name me the names of all
the faces you've got for show and tell
when you're up in the sky.
I have but one
face, this one and only.
In daylight it shows, it tells a whole
story of regret.

I can't disappear like you
when night goes. Come morning,
here I'll be, in broad day, watching
you make a clean escape—
your pale smudge left
like some faint
moustache of milk on the hard
blue sky.

HIGH RISK

What of myself could I give you?
What flower of longing, what deep tight
outtake of sigh and regret?
What exhalation, what halo
of breath, circle and spike,
looping ray, this breath
as I float toward
sleep's offshore wave?

Perhaps your interests lie nearer
the bone. My bones.
These opal translucents, these uprights
of courage, racks of necessity.
Fretted, misaligned: the frame
my flesh so cleverly mimes.

What of this self could I
give you today? I close my eyes.
A pinprick of light moves
across the blood-blackness
inside my sight.
Are you with me now?
Call it streak of heat,
a single star, falling flame:
brief, unreliable. Tell me
if I'm close. Ask for it by name.

IN PRAISE

I raise my hands above my head
and see the tell-tale blood
disappear. Praise.
The veins that rope the back of my hands:
gone. Whatever, wherever I touch
is a drum. Countertop, cupboard door,
a window's smooth stare—all backbeat
and beat at the throb of my fingers. All praise.

Even delirious, reeling, I dance.
My arms reach for this room
to pull the shadowed walls toward me.
Lintel, wainscot, frame and sash,
sweep them all in. I could bite
the inside of my mouth
in two. I could.

I'll marry the moon instead—
on the fourth finger of my left hand,
a huge opal, wedding gift
from this love, the moon.
I'll dance his wedding dance,
two-step with this silvery one
whose ears are wound with burnished snakes.
Wine pours from between his lips,
a stream, red and clear.
Flames that surround his mouth
lick at his cheekbones and chin.
His eyebrows flare up and up,
ascending the night sky.
He'll dance with me—this moon, here
in his body of pleasure.
I'm alive in the heaven of my own
making. I dance on vermilion,
each step stirring cinnabar dust,
swirling it round and around. In praise.

Music stains the night,
no sleep, no sleep.
An opal moon on my left hand
ringing the place
where the marriage should be,
I fall into bed with my clothes on,
purple winding my body,
whole cloth of my passage
into tomorrow.
I could fall forever before
my lips touched a thing.

Moon in my bed,
and my body unmoored.
A taste of blood in this breath.
Lips now mouthing the words, wine-sweet,
perfume in their making,
to say this praise.

MIRACLE

The wonder isn't that lightning
strikes where it does, but that it doesn't
strike everywhere. Specifically me.
It isn't the frequency of car crashes,
but their infrequency. Traffic flicks along
in its speed and perplexity, each move,
each surge a potential disaster.

The heart beats out its strange
litany of the enormously possible,
never excluding disease and stricture.
Why does my blood run so easy and warm?
This is the wonder: me approaching
the traffic light just turned yellow,
my foot pressing my trust down
into the brake, the car in agreement
coming steady steady to a stop.

TO LOVE MY OWN

Only late do I learn to touch
my body. Only later, with this body
purged of its womb, do I see
a belly swollen with child as a shape
for caress, a curve for clothes
to mold. Stretch marks are the faint
crescents of daylight moon
risen onto her skin
when a pregnant woman bares
herself to sun. Lately I have
come to call what I once called *modesty*
by its true name: *shame* deep
and wordless for the shapes
a woman's body takes. I gaze with joy
at the friend seven months along
whose jersey dress stretches around
every swing of her breasts and belly,
whose husband slides his hand like a sling
under their child's weight to feel
its kick and turn. With fingertip,
I trace the opal streaks where my skin
stretched away from itself as my babies
grew heavy within me.
I finger without dismay
the still tender rope of scar
marking where I was emptied
of that womb. In late ripeness, I learn.

III.

An Animal's Making

Bee sting—nugget of flame
trapped under my skin—
you struggle toward the air.

All your red, a furious burr,
reaches out for your twin,
the one who carries

a weight of yellow dust—
the twin already dying,
already flown away.

SONG FOR THE ONE
WHO WAITS IN THE FOREST

Woman in the pines, I bring you
a gift, branch of wild plums,
the white bloom of dusk
still warm on their skins.

Woman who waits in quaking aspen,
I sought you in April but found
hollow morels, their gaping scent
filling my breath with spore.

I came to you once as a girl offering
a bread of citron wrapped in crisp paper,
a folded blue fan, afraid to turn
my back to your eyes.

Forest one, snowbanks have melted,
water is rushing me into
its cleft. When I fall, you must
promise to swallow the sound.

CHTHONIC

Near the steps on the strip of broken
pavement where I'm headed to park my car,
a flicker. Its beak into and into the cracks
so a little fine dirt flies.
Ants or grubs, no telling. Nothing shows
but the stab, stab, the arc as he leans
into it, arching his back with enough force
to send his tail into a downward curve,
fierce little hoop of intent.
So I watch from behind the wheel,
the car sideways in the street, pointed at
the driveway—stalled by fascination
with this woodpecker working the crevices,
delving into an under world.

Later, as I lie down with a book,
my eyes follow my length. Along the folds
and broken lines of cloth, I see
thin worms of petal and leaf
my body gathered while I picked flowers
this last hour. If I lie like this—
flat, ever so still, the line of me
made uneven by this jut and jag of bones,
by the rumpled cloth that wraps itself
around my body like familiarity
wraps around a place of sleep—
will a flicker walk across me,
prying these worms from my flesh?
In the kingdom of death there is at least
one live body—mine, flourishing toward it.

MAGNOLIA

❧

Globe of petals big as a moon
translucent, shining, most ancient of flowers
I pin in the back of my hair.
Cream magnolia veined with purple
that seeps a sweetmilk perfume,
sheds a pollen down into tangled hair.

❧

Maybe it's the magnolia. What else
could make the young man in that shop—
the much younger man with his thin, flannel
collarless shirt buttoned at the throat—
what else could make him ask
my name? Midway in the warbler green
of a song he's singing, he stops long enough
to ask me my name,
and starts again when I've answered,
then stops when I move away,
beginning yet another
complicated tune as I drift
back into his view.

❧

Heading toward the park, maybe
it's that tune that makes the air
impossibly clear, weightless with the press
of every possible bit of light.
A complicated tune
floats my steps along an asphalt path—
meandering path through the park's
open ground where people
scatter themselves to picnic and play
like cotton from some great tree,
moving in gentle fits and starts
across the slow swells of lawn.

I walk this path behind two women,
mother and daughter, perhaps. Both old.
The mother's hair flies down her back
in a shock of white. Stiff legs jerking along,
she walks with her lock-kneed legs
spread apart, her whole body taking—side to side—
the jolt of each step.
She holds her arms in front of her,
feeling the way as if she were blind,
beating out the rhythm of what's to come,
walk of a mummy trailing
the long echo of bandages.
She points, exclaims, blurts out, but to what
I can't tell. Matching slow step
for slow step, the daughter leans in, murmurs
in the old woman's ear. Now and again
they hold hands, and I follow
in their gentle wake.

ཡ
The air this time of year
must be filled with the gold of pollen.
The three of us are breathing in
huge eddies of pollen with every breath.
My legs are liquid, my torso
buoyant with tenderness,
the ache of unmet desire.
Today as I move—this way, that way,
whatever way I will—
my body doesn't rub any air
the wrong way. My body
meets the air in just this exact way:
soundless, easy.

ⓞ
The grave might be a shallow thing—
no more than a bit of uneven ground
strewn thick with the glint of pollen.
This day I know that someday
I'll lie down, unbidden,
in the long and deepening
bed of broken flowers.

BLACKBERRY WOUND

Thick. The juice we share
in our favorite bakery's clamor
is thick enough to clot, to cling
to his fingertip after he's run it along
the bottle's smooth inside.

He's already made his toasts—paper cup
to paper cup—*To love,* he says, *to union
and connection, to sweet, stolen kisses.*
He's asked for my toast, and I've already tried
to say what only at a later moment
will I know how to say: *Here's to the wilderness
of being together and then being
apart.* His fingertip is against my lips,
now into my mouth, pressing
the berry's sweetness against my tongue.
Again and again he feeds me from what remains
until I too press a finger, a berry kiss into him.
We suck the fragrance of heat and bramble
from each other's skin.

His fingertip on the bottle's rim brings away
an even streak of red. *A cut,* I say,
and he replies, *a blackberry wound,*
then gives it to my mouth.

A drop has fallen onto a napkin
at our table's edge. Now the white paper
takes this little shock, feeds it into itself,
fiber by fiber. We rise to leave. Glancing down
a last time, he fixes the spot in his eyes.
Blood on a sheet, he says—a single
drop of blood. *On a marriage bed*
are the words we each think
and both choose not to speak.

DEEP IN THE PLEASURES
OF EARTHLY HABIT

If ever I smoke tobacco again,
let it be in a pipe whose bowl
is shaped like an animal's body.
Let the smoke I take
into my body come by way
of the animal world.

Oh, what a fine and high
buzzing that smoke will make
at home in my blood—
my breath drawn through the leafy depth
of an animal cradled in my hand,
my being seared by the fire
alive at its heart.

PROVISIONS

Redwing blackbirds feed
on sunflowers bent
halfway to the ground.
Hanging upside down,
they pluck and crack
dark seeds, slowly blinding
each flower's heavy eye.

I want to tell them
Wait, it's only October,
leave some seeds until
much later when
you'll need them more.

They whistle a liquid pleasure
at my niggle of caution,
my woodpile of lodgepole and fir—

they, with feathers spread
blacker than frozen stone,
with shoulders already
mantled in blood.

SONG OF THE EARLY, WARM WIND

I come from the land where sibling winds
meet head-on, battering themselves
into silence. Born from that stand-off,
I move toward a place where cold
has fallen and stayed, my path
as long as white can take to disappear.

Along the way, my eyes devour
shade, shadow, the brightness that ice
wears as its cloak and muffler.
I like the moan of melting,
not its sharp touch. Mantled by
what's spoken, I fall silent
to questions, listening instead
for the sough and rill of my name,
Chinook, *the Snow-Eater.*

RETROSPECT

To say *dusk* is to fall short
of telling how only a coral tinge
remained on the sky, how the wind
had stilled itself to coax
meadow scent from the canal.
Our dog ran tight circles around us.
Black-crowned night herons
flushed at our approaching steps,
then returned to glide
a few feet over our heads.

We had little sense of our bodies.
Only midges tangling in our hair,
a ditchbank's uneven ground
underfoot, the air's steady
loss of heat. Lacking the power
to imagine anything's absence,
we walked. Herons startled and flew.
A killdeer rose with her familiar
ki-ree, ki-ree, and we barely
took notice—even though moment
by moment our eyes grew large,
their apertures wide enough to admit
most of the darkening world.

SIGHTSEEING

These trees are on fire, always
have been, the invention of green
simply the offspring
of modest longing, this color
a mere disguise for steady
blaze. Crane your neck—
nothing but this metaphor
will do—crane it toward
the slough where herons might be,
and you see one,
lone on a hummock of grasses
that rise from the water's
flat pewter sheen. What other
shape hooks earth to air
in this exact way: the neck
a glyph, a flicker of fire gone
half sashaying to heaven?
These trees stacked along water's edge,
licking themselves upward, branch
by branch, are as much aflame
as this bird you sight
through heat waves buckling
air before your eyes.

WHAT THE MOON LEAVES UNDONE

—after Pissarro

Morning sun is a soft
palm on the landscape's brow,
long silk of fingers draped over,
soothing each color
out of focus. Early morning
is the spectrum of blur,
each hue broken, diffused
into its thousand neighbors: color
scattered out along a roof's slope,
the hedge's countless asides,
a pinking shear edge of leaf.
What is blue, then violet is quickly
rosy rushing toward yellow,
while the blue-black of shadow
lays lanky fingers of its own
across the roll of ground.
Longest at dawn, strips of shade
escape from each tree trunk's base,
then shorten, harden into the thick black
demanded by ascending sun.
The field's cow pushes its legs
through a fanfare of grass, pulling
a sprinkled shadow along behind.
Like the dark side of the moon
thrown down, made visible,
this shadow sidles in. Minute
by climbing-sun minute,
it moves a little closer to
its source, its twin.

ICE FISHERMEN

On the long drive to Hyatt Lake,
they trade bits of recurring dreams.
One makes thirty foot leaps,
another floats beyond the reach
of a curved blade, a third falls
from great heights in great fear until
he remembers he'll land ok.
He hits the ground with a jolt
and wakes up.

Thermos, lawn chair,
plastic bucket around each hole,
and the ice floor making its
barrel-belly groans.
Poles set, the men walk to get warm,
talking about Velveeta,
treble hooks, cleated boots,
the daylight that's left, the best
depth to try for another
flash of what quickens that world
just below their reach.

YES, WALT WHITMAN

The grass is indeed itself
a child, child of a fir whose scabbed trunk
lifts needles of resin into the sun,
child of a stenciled oak lunging
at the wind. You say, then science repeats
that grass is the offspring of trees.
Trees evolved to thin blades,
huge grows into small,
and all our belief that little
moves inexorably toward big
vanishes with the rest of school's
unraveled lessons.

The skies grow into a mouthful
of air, the mountain into a temple
reflected on the river's eye.
Pounding and pounding, the ocean
turns itself to a blaze of salt,
while the sun keeps busy becoming
the work of bees—chambers of honey
housed in an animal's skull.

Our bodies too—knuckle and shank,
twists of muscle and hair—
have come from another
bodied forth huge and fine.
Children of such expanse, we, in turn,
are growing toward something
much smaller yet fine—
small as the stone of a summer fruit,
blood cherry: its hard seed a size
to be carried unseen, pressed between
finger and thumb.

TRICKSTER

I saw a crow
dive into a grove of twisted oak,

ancient trees rimed
with lichen—

seaweed oak, its bark rough
with brackish crust,

briny with that greenlessness
of the deepest deep.

Of the crow's sheen,
its dark gleam,

not a sign
in those branches of salt-rind.

I saw a jay emerge flying.
Blue. Sleek as a wave's wing.

FALLING STARS

The thicketed stars struck up
conversations with distance,
their brief, hot scratches curved
against the sky's dome.
Zipped into a sleeping bag,
high on a bluff above the river,
I turned my face toward
this one direction of wonder.
Friction suddenly visible,
life burned itself out in streaking arcs
far above my eyes. Yet I couldn't
keep from turning away.

           Off to one side,
rising from the opposite bluff:
the huge moon, fat crescent.
Succulent cream of a moon,
big as a wide, wild
animal yawn held open
on the horizon. Risen, still rising,
and I, who'd never before wanted
to sleep in the open, chose to stay.
Outside my familiar landscape
of wallpaper, curtains, doors,
I could hear the coyotes
throw their great circle of cries
up into the air, two owls criss and cross
their voices through trees;
I could turn from moon to stars
to moon, watch them to sleep,
rouse to see them again, and go again
back to sleep in that wide outside;
then wake in morning to find
the sleeping bag, my face, hands
wet and shining with what, at dawning,
fell to the ground.

DEAD CENTERED

At work in my garden, I haven't time
to be too distracted by what I find
on a pathway's hard-packed dirt: a mouse,
small and dead. Why I dread
to touch it barehanded remains
unexplained, but it's not something
to leave for the cat's toying,
so I turn a heavy clay flowerpot
upside down to cover it.

Just the dull red of clay
ringed with salts from watering,
simply a thing overturned
on the pathway I walk.
And I don't walk that way for a day
or two, or forget, or maybe both,
but it's true the sight of that flowerpot
days later gives me a start.
Why I lift the pot so gingerly
is a mystery, why I set it quick
back down in the same spot
is not. That tiny carcass is alive,
seething with ants, busy with secret
comings and goings.

After days more of me going
about my business—the flowerpot
nudged at the edge of my eye—
I finally squat and lift it away again
to find that small creature
even smaller, taken down,
gone white: a skeleton
curling dead center in its ring
of faintly darkened earth.
Bloom of finest bone.

CONVERT

Kneeling in the garden I gasp
at a tight whir near
my ear, and raise my face
to a hummingbird
eye to eye
hovering stark still—
except for its wing-blur.

In the next intake
of breath I believe
what before I merely
thought I believed: a man's story
of his mother—her lips
painted poppy-red,
a hummingbird come
close enough to sip
honey from her tongue.

A SACRAMENT

Become that high priest,
the bee. Drone your way
from one fragrant
temple to another, nosing
into each altar. Drink
what's divine—
and while you're there,
let some of the sacred
cling to your limbs.
Wherever you go
leave a small trail
of its golden crumbs.

In your wake
the world unfolds
its rapture, the fruit
of its blooming.
Rooms in your house
fill with that sweetness
your body both
makes and eats.

FROM WHAT'S MOST SOFT, TREES CARRY ON

May, and the fat-leaved
trees let loose their cotton.
In wisps and tufts,
it carries along on the slightest
shudder of air.

The green world's deep fur
is white as light,
as sunwash. Inside each bit
of this belly-down,
a seed floats.

THIRST

Your eyes must stay open
to the color of flowers.
Wherever their bright flash
catches your gaze, water flows.

You see rain
days after it stopped raining.
In your breath, you taste
the river running underground.

REPLENISH

Last night the rain held me under
a roof of sound. The night long,
rain hung its murmur over my sleep.
Dreams came and fled, each
a night-opening bloom
that shut itself back into bud
before morning arrived.

My breath and heartbeat followed
a simple-minded routine,
in, out, pull, give way.
Part of me grew
a little, more of me sank,
the lost were mostly replaced.
Rain fed whatever was mine.

WILDCRAFT

—for Denise Levertov

Crossing a forest stream to reach
more huckleberries, I walk
on a beaver dam,
tightroping its narrow rim,
and think of you a continent away,
how you'd like
this springy mesh of branches and twigs
that stretches across to make—with the
hesitation it creates—
a pond upstream, a small
spillway down.

I imagine you here—
your laugh, that girlish shriek,
as you teeter to miss
little surprises of grass and wildflower
strung along our path,
the dam's only surface that stays
in contact with air.

Stopped to look at what must be
beaver scat
slowly breaking apart on the bottom
of the clear, shallow pond,
we hear a grouse pipe its ventriloquial call.
There.
There.
And there.
We know its crop is packed
with huckleberries,
the same dark tartness
that shadows our lips and hands.

I tell you this balancing act—
   one hand holding a pail half full of berries
      the other flung out
         while I place one foot, then the other
           on this spongy contraption's
   one walkable line—
       is like writing a poem. You say,
              better yet
       look at the beaver dam itself:
   an animal's making.
 You love
how its weave of branches, roots and silt
    holds us—
   both holds and lets the water go.

PRAGMATICS

In your story of bees,
they slowly fill an outside wall—
three stud-spaces wide, two storeys high—
in the front bay of your old farmhouse.
You first try all the poisons,

even your pickup set
to run all day, its exhaust
piped into a hole in the wall—
while you go away, hoping the fumes
will kill them. But no.

So on a winter's icy morning
you pull the siding off
and scrape out, storey by tall storey,
thick clots of comb and honey,
clumps of stiff, chilled bees.

They had to go. No question.
But tell me again, please,
how you stood inside and breathed—
in summer's reckless heat—
the fragrance of their work,

wild perfume of wax and flower.
Say again how you pressed your ear
tight to the wall, heard the house humming,
its blur of countless wings
a fine, even tremble.

IN LONG SUPPLY

For the object of desire,
consider the Inexhaustible
Purse, the well without a word
for dry, an eight lying
on its side to take
a delectable Vishnu nap—
consider only what comes
in infinite supply.

Dream the world alive
without those two sets of hands
both intent on gaining
a single prize. Dream the hands,
by all means do,
but dream into being
prizes beyond number.
No ante, no trump.
No winner take all
when the prize can be a *be-all*
with no end.

Confound the maker of odds
by wanting what's common enough
to have no limit: the little twigs
of coincidence, the grit of joy
under your feet, words that trail
from your lips like haphazard
banners in the wind.

Acknowledgements

These poems (some in earlier versions) first appeared or are scheduled to appear in the following publications:

The Alembic: "Reprieve"
The Animal Bride (Trask House Books, 1994): "Manifesto;" "In Praise;" "Yes, Walt Whitman"
Beloit Poetry Journal: "Under the Sign of a Neon Wolf"
Blue Unicorn: "Moles"
Calapooya Collage: "Dead-Centered;" "For a Season's Keeping"
Calyx: "Lane Change"
Carolina Quarterly: "What the Moon Leaves Undone"
Chaffin Journal: "Acrimony"
Departed: Poems on Fathers and Loss (edited by Meghan Adler): "Maintain"
Fabrication (26 Books, 1996): "Falling Stars;" "Magnolia;" "One-Sided Conversation with the Moon;" "A Vapor, It Rises at Waking;" "High Risk"
Fireweed: "Branch Library;" "In Long Supply;" "Retrospect;" "Salvage;" "Scour;" "Restorer"
The Grove Review: "A Sacrament," "From What's Most Soft, Trees Carry On," "Thirst"
Heliotrope: "Trickster"
Hubbub: "In Praise"
The Ledge: "Black"
Manzanita Quarterly: "Convert;" "Stones;" "Chthonic;" "Grant Court;" "A Last, Cool Thing"
National Forum: "His Map Unfolding" (as "A Father's Map Unfolding")
Northwest Poets and Artists Calendar, 1989: "The House at 4 AM"
Open Spaces: "Replenish"
Oregon English Journal: "White Lie"
Pearl: "Deep in the Pleasures of Earthly Habit"
Poetry: "Primed"
Poetry Northwest: "A Vapor, It Rises at Waking;" "Collision"
Prairie Schooner: "Miracle"
Sojourner: "My Father, Hard at the Work of Early Summer;" "To Love My Own"
Twelve Oregon Poets 2: "High Risk"
Under the Sign of a Neon Wolf (Confluence Press, 1989): "For A Season's Keeping;" "Under the Sign of a Neon Wolf;" "Moles;" "Wildcraft"
Weber Studies: "Ice Fishermen;" "Sightseeing;" "Wildcraft;" "Yes, Walt Whitman"
West Wind Review: "Provisions"
Wildsong: (University of Georgia Press, 1998): "Pragmatics"
Wilderness Magazine: "Convert"
Windfall: "Song of the Early, Warm Wind"

I thank Greg Simon for his inspired advice, and those in the Pearls, Odd Mondays, and Poetry Church groups for their astute responses to earlier versions of some of these poems.

To Tony Gorsline, Peter Sears, Michael Malan, Roberta Sperling, and Brandon Conn—the Cloudbank Clan, I offer my gratitude. I admire their dedication to the publication of poetry, and I'm indebted to them for their faith in my work.

Paulann Petersen's previous publications include two full-length collections of poems—*Blood Silk* from Quiet Lion Press, and *The Wild Awake* from Confluence Press; and three chapbooks—*Fabrication* from 26 Books, *The Animal Bride* from Trask House Press, and *Under the Sign of a Neon Wolf* from Confluence Press. Her work has been anthologized in *From Here We Speak, An Anthology of Oregon Poetry*; *Claiming the Spirit Within*; *The Anthology of Magazine Verse and Yearbook of American Poetry*; *O Poetry! Oh Poesia! Poems of Oregon and Peru*; *Florilegia*; and *Wildsong*.

A former Stegner Fellow at Stanford University and the winner of two Carolyn Kizer Awards, she has been on the faculty for the Creative Arts Community at Menucha, and has given workshops for Oregon Writers Workshop, Oregon State Poetry Association, and Mountain Writers Series. As a board member for Friends of William Stafford, she organizes the annual January Stafford Birthday Events.

About the Publishers

Bedbug Press was founded in 1995 by Tony Gorsline, who has had a life-long love of books and writing. His inaugural publishing effort was *Going Over the Falls*, a collection of poetry, by Gretchen Sousa.

The name Cloudbank Books was established in 2000 by Peter Sears and Michael Malan with the publication of *Millennial Spring—Eight New Oregon Poets*.

Cloudbank Books became an imprint of Bedbug Press in 2002. Since that time, Bedbug Press has established, under its Cloudbank imprint, the Northwest Poetry Series and The Rhea & Seymour Gorsline Poetry Competition. In 2005, *Woman in the Water: A Memoir of Growing Up in Hollywood*, by Dorinda Clifton, was published by Bedbug Press. *Woman in the Water* is a creative non-fiction memoir. It is our hope that all of the Bedbug/Cloudbank books express our commitment to quality in writing and publishing.